Dr. H. S. McNaughety

English
Grammar and other Shit

Ein nicht ganz sauberer Englisch-Kurs

Eichborn.

Dr. McNaughety wishes to express his thanks to his learned and astute colleagues Michèle (the Bimbo) Mens, Mr. Mei Catherall (Oxford man, you know), and the elusive Mr. Friedberg for their assistance and encouragement. Special thanks also to Missus M.Q.-S. for casting a critical eye at the manuscript.

Die Deutsche Bibliothek – CIP-Einheitsaufnahme

McNaughety, H. S.:
English Grammar and other Shit : ein nicht ganz sauberer Englisch-Kurs /
Dr. McNaughety. – Frankfurt am Main : Eichborn, 1996
ISBN 3-8218-3409-9

Umschlaggestaltung: Rüdiger Morgenweck unter Verwendung
einer Zeichnung von Stephan Hagenow.
Gesamtherstellung: Fuldaer Verlagsanstalt GmbH.
ISBN 3-8218-3409-9
Verlagsverzeichnis schickt gern:
Eichborn Verlag, Kaiserstraße 66, 60329 Frankfurt am Main

The pen is mightier than the sword.
– Edward Bulwer-Lytton
(1803-1873)

The penis mightier than the sword.
– Mark Twain
(1835-1910)

MR.
BIG

Table of contents
Inhaltsverzeichnis

Introduction

Wie kann ich sinnvoll lernen und wiederholen?

1.
Vokabeln üben

Erster Schritt: Vokabeln einschreiben

a) Du solltest unbedingt ein Vokabelheft führen.
   Dr. McNaughety empfiehlt Größe DIN A4.
b) Du findest ein Glossar am Ende des Buches.
c) Teile die Seiten deines Vokabelheftes in 3 Spalten ein.

1. Spalte	2. Spalte	3. Spalte
das neue englische Wort	das neue Wort im Zusammenhang	die deutsche Bedeutung
Shorts	**Eat my shorts.**	**Leck mich.**
Flying fuck	**Go take a flying fuck.**	**Verpiß dich. Zieh' Leine.**
Woody	**to sport a woody**	**einen Ständer haben**

Zweiter Schritt: Vokabeln lernen

a) Lies alle drei Spalten laut.
b) Decke die Spalten 1 und 3 ab und sage den vollständigen Satz.
c) Präge dir den Beispielsatz von Spalte 2 ein.
d) Decke nun Spalte 3 ab und sage die deutsche Übersetzung.
e) Decke dann die Spalten 1 und 2 ab und schreibe das englische Wort auf deinen Übungsblock.
f) Wenn du Rechtschreibfehler gemacht hast, schreibe die betreffenden Wörter mehrmals an und präge sie dir ein.

Dritter Schritt: Vokabeln wiederholen

a) Nimm dir einen festen Zeitpunkt vor, um Vokabeln zu wiederholen, z.B. nach jeder Lektion oder jeden Samstag.
b) Du wirst häufig feststellen, daß du Wörter vergessen hast bzw. bei etlichen unsicher bist. Kennzeichne diese Wörter mit einem Bleistift oder Textmarker.
c) Du mußt diese Problemwörter nun erneut üben.
d) Vor Schulaufgaben oder Tests kannst du deine Problemwörter, vor allem solche, die du bereits mehrfach angekreuzt und wiederholt hast, so schneller in den Griff bekommen.

Chapter 1: The Parts of Speech

The Private Parts

The Breasts

Apples
Bags
Balboas
Balloons
Bassoons
Bazongas
Bazooms
Bazoonjies
Beacons
Big brown eyes
Blossoms
Boobies
Boobs
Bosom
Boulders
Breastworks
Bubbas
Bumpers
Bust
Cannon balls
Cans
Cantaloupes
Casabas
Cha-chas
Charlies
Coconuts
Congas
Cream-pies
Creamers
Cupcakes
Dagmars
Diddies
Dingers
Dingos
Domes
Doodads
Doozies
Droopers
Dugs
Dumplings
Ear muffs
Flappers
Floaters
Floppers
Fog lights

Garbonzas
Garbos
Gazongas
Glands
Globes
Grillwork
Handsets
Handwarmers
Headers
Headlamps
Headlights
Headphones
Headsets
Hemispheres
Hillocks of love
Honeydews
Honkers
Hoohahs
Hooters
Hubcaps
Humdingers
Hushpuppies
Jawbreakers
Jemimas
Jibs
Jobbers
Jugs
Jukes
Jumbos
Kazongas
Kazoos
Knobs
Knockers
Lactoids
Love bags
Love melons
Love muffins
Love pillows
Lulus
Lungs
Mambos
Melons
Milk cans
Milk fountains
Milkers
Milkshakes
Mounds
Muffins
Mulligans
Nancies
Nay-nays
Niblets
Nippeloons
Nippers
Nips
Nodes
Orbs
Orbs of love
Ottomans
Pagodas
Pair
Papayas
Pastries
Peaches
Peaks
Pears

Pects
Pillows
Pips
Plums
Pointers
Pokers
Polygons
Pompoms
Pontoons
Pups
Rangoons
Rib cushions
Rocks
Sandbags
Set
Shakers
Silos
Skooners
Snorbs
Snuggle pups
Spheres
Stacks
Sweater meat
Sweet rolls
Tatas
Teats
Tits
Titskis
Titties
Tomatoes

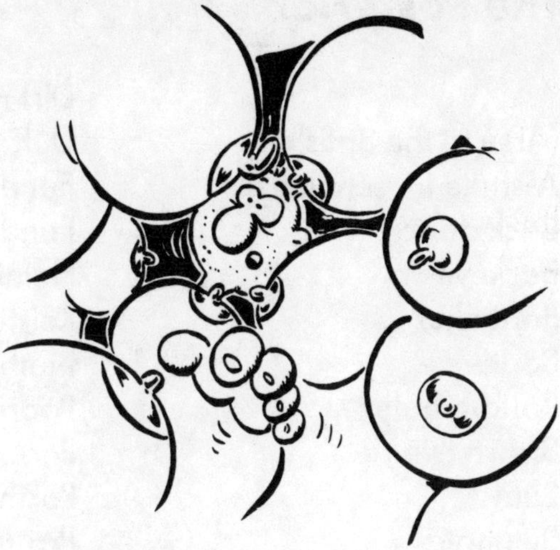

Tweeters
Twin peaks
Udders
Wahwahs
Waldos
Watermelons
Whoppers
Wobblers
Wombats
Wongas
Woofers
Yabos
Yams
Zeppelins
Zingers

The Posterior

Ass
(Arse to the Britisher)
Asshole (Arsehole)
Back door
Backeye
Bohunkus
Bootie
Bottom-hole
Brown eye
Bum
Bumhole
Bung
Bunghole
Buns
Butt
Butthole
Buttocks
Can
Cornhole
Culo
Derrière
Dirt chute
Dirt road
Duff
Fundament
Fundus
Heinie
Keister
Nether hole
Poop chute
Pooper
Porthole
Prat(t)
Rosebud
Roundeye
Rump
Scut
Shitter
Tail
Tradesman's entrance
Tush
Tushy
Vent hole
Ying-yang

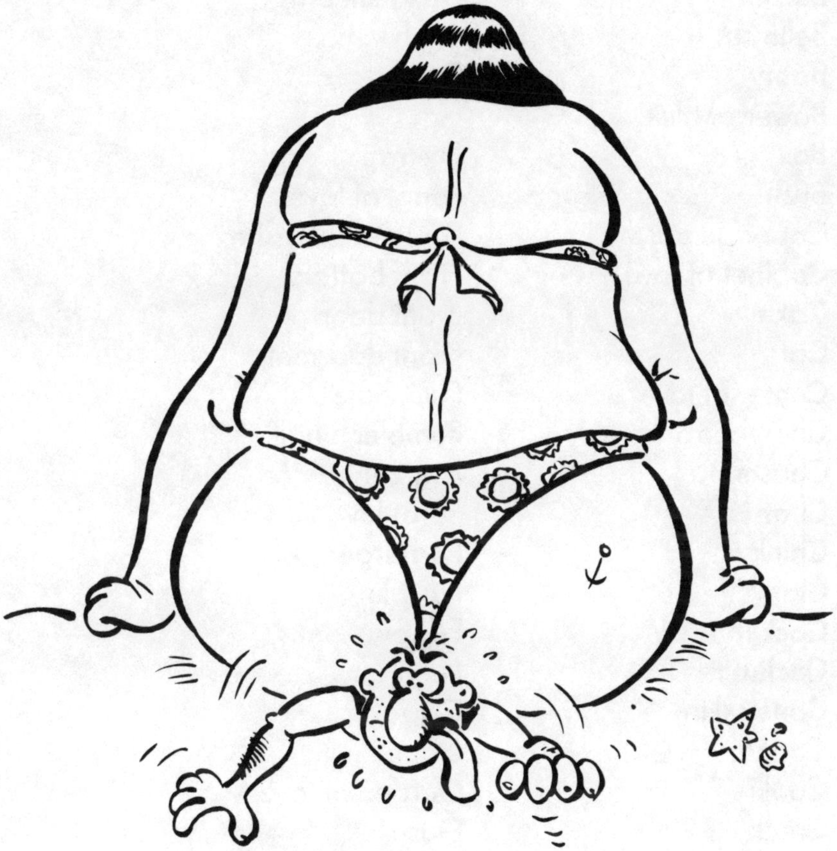

The Vagina

Ass
Baking pot
Bearded clam
Beaver
Belle chose
Booty
Bower of bliss
Box
Bush
Cabbage patch
Cabinet of love
Cake
Cat
Center of love
Chamber of love
Chasm
Chat
Chink
Clam
Cock Inn
Cockshire
Coney skin
Coochy
Cookie
Crack
Cranny
Crater
Cream jug
Crevice
Cunny
Cunny-warren
Cunt
Cupid's alley
Cupid's furrow
Dewy sheath
Ditch
Fanny
Fig
Fly trap
Fount of love
Fount of pleasure
Front bottom
Front door
Front doormat
Fuck-hole
Fumbler's hall
Fun-zone
Furbelow
Furburger
Fur-pie
Furrow
Futy
Gap
Gape
Garden of love
Gash
Gate of life
Gate of love
Gates of Paradise
Gentleman's pleasure garden
Great Divide
Grindstone

Grotto of love
Grotto of Venus
Gulf
Gulley
Gulley-hole
Hair pie
Hairy Mary
Hairy oyster
Hairyfordshire
Harbor of Cytheria
Harbor of love
Haven of love
Hole
Hole of content
Holiday Inn
Honey-pie

Honey-pot
House under the hill
Jam
Jelly
Jellyroll
Jinny
Joy-furrow
Kennel
Kitty
Lady's water-box
Lady's water-engine
Lady's water gap
Lady's water gate
Lady's water mill
Lady's water-works
Lady Jane
Lather-maker
Leg
Love-box
Love chink
Love-cleft
Love Lane
Love-nest
Love-niche
Love-organ
Love-sheath
Love-spot
Love-tunnel
Love's pavilion
Lower mouth
Lunch
Man-eater
Man-trap

Maw
Mine of pleasure
Money-spinner
Moniche
Mossy grotto
Mot
Motte
Mount of Venus
Mouse
Mouse's hole
Mousehole
Muff
Nether beard
Nick
Nookie
Notch
Organ of bliss

"P"
Path of bliss
Path of joy
Pelt
Piece of ass
Pink altar
Pit
Placket
Playground
Playpen
Poontang
Poozle
Porthole
Pretty Polly
Pud
Puffer
Puss
Pussy
Quiff
Quim
Rosebud
Sanctum of love
Seat of bliss
Seat of joy
Seat of love
Seat of paradise
Seat of pleasure
Sheath
Shrine of love
Slash
Slit
Slot
Snatch
Stuff
Sugarbush
Tail
Temple of love
Temple of Venus
Thing
Throne of felicity
Treasure box
Trench
Trim
Tunnel of love
Twat
Upright grin
Venus' Fly Trap
Venus' wrinkle
Vertical smile
Welcome mat
Whetting-corne
Wrinkle of love

The Penis

Adam's needle
Affair
Arrow of love
Baldheaded candidate
Banger
Battering ram
Beanpole
Beanstalk
Beef javelin
Big dipper
Bodkin
Bone
Bozack
Broadsword
Carrot
Cock
Codpiece
Column
Corkscrew
Coupling bat
Courser
Crank
Cream horn
Cream-stick
Cupid's battering ram
Cupid's dart
Dart of love
Derrick
Dick
Diddler
Dingus

Dipstick
Dong
Doodle
Dork
Dr. Johnson
Engine of love
Fiddling stick
Flute
Fountain of pleasure
Fuckpole
Fuck-stick
Game-cock
Goober
Hog
Instrument
Jacob's staff
Jewel of pleasure
Jim
Jimbrowski
Jimmy
Jimmy joint
Jock
John Henry Longfellow
John Thomas
John Willie
Johnson
Joint
Jones
Joystick
Kennedy (= Schürhaken)
Kennel-raker
Knob
Lance

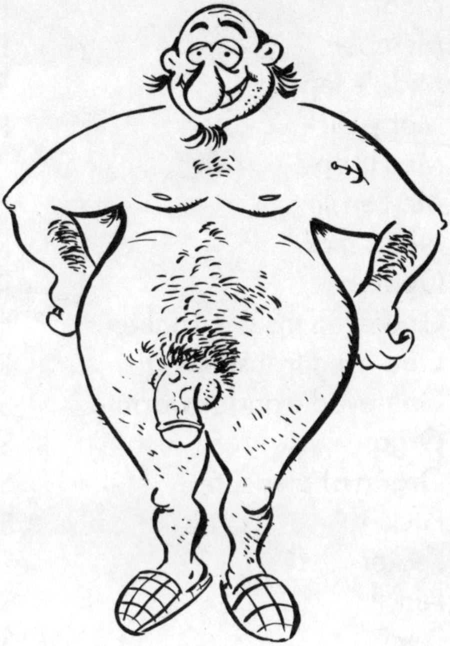

Little friend
Little Richard
Love-gun
Love machine
Love-muscle
Love pump
Love sceptre
Love-stick
Love-wand
Love's piston-rod
Mandrake
Manhood
Man-meat
Man Thomas

Meat
Member
Middle leg
Moby Dick
Mr. Happy
Mr. Peaslin
Night stick
Obelisk
One-eyed trouser snake
One-eyed trouser trout
One-eyed wonder worm
Organ
Organ of pleasure
Packet
Pecker
Pencil
Percy
Pet snake
Peter
Piddler
Pikestaff
Pipe
Pisser
Piss-pipe
Piston
Pizzle
Plonker
Plooker
Poker
Pole
Pork sword
Poser
Post of lust
Priapus
Prick
Pud
Pumphandle
Purple throbber
Putz
Rig
Rod
Rogering iron
Root
Salami
Schlong
Screwdriver
Shaft
Shaft of love
Shooting iron
Shooting stick
Shunter's pole
Spear of love
Staff d'amour

Staff of life
Stuff
Sugar-stick
Tally-whacker
Tassel
The Devil's dizen
The iron sausage
The old fella
The old gentleman
The old man
Third leg
Throbber
Tickler
Tiddler
Tool
Tool of generation
Tosser
Tree of love
Trouser mouse
Truncheon
Tube snake
Tube steak
Unit
Vade mecum of pleasure
Wang
Wanger
Wankus
Weapon of love
Weenie
Wicked Willie
Willy
Worm
Yard

The Testicles

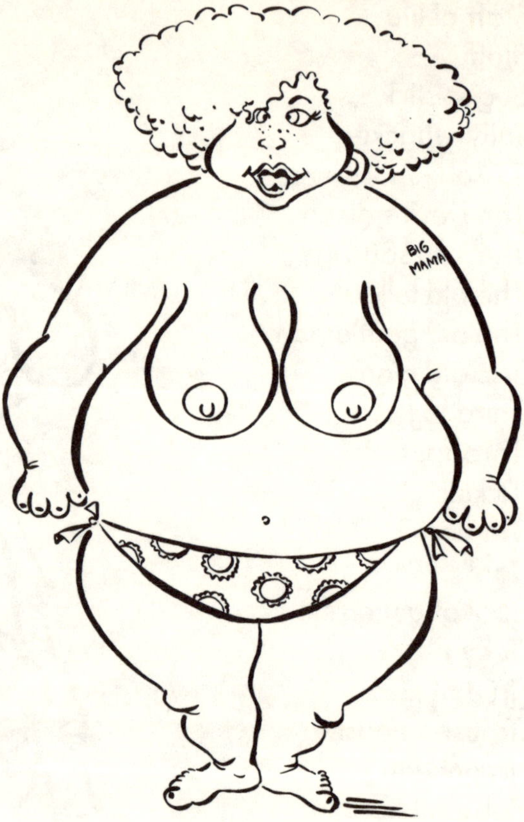

Apples
Ballocks
Balls
Bollicks
Cobblers
Cods
Cojones
Dusters
Family jewels
Huevos
Ladies' jewels
Marbles
Nuts
Reservoirs of love
Rocks
Stones

Copulation

A homer
A homerun
A push up the bush
A put in
Coition
Combat of love
Love engagement
Operation leg-wrap
The merry feat
to ball
to bang
to be bonin'
to be makin' bacon
to be united
to boff
to boink
to bone
to bone-dance
to bonk
to bump
to bump fuzz
to bun

to copulate (with)
to diddle
to do a bottom wetter
to do a knee-trembler
to do a perpindicular
to do a wet one
to do a whisker-splitter
to do the deed
to do the do
to do the nasty
to do the thing
to do the wild thing
to dork or get dorked
to enjoy
to fettle
to frig
to fuck
to get a leg over
to get a piece
to get a piece of ass
to get a piece of tail
to get a shot of leg
to get bred
to get fucked
to get hosed
to get it on
to get laid
to get one's
ashes hauled
to get one's greens
to get over
(with someone)
to get some
to get some ass
to get some booty
to get some gash
to get some honey
on one's stinger
to get some leg
to get some tail
to give it up
to give up the ass
to go all the way
to go to the limit
to go tummy tickling
to grease the wheel
to grind
to have a bout
to have a poke
to have a shie
to have it away
to have it off
to have it up
to have one's end off
to hide the salami
to hit a homerun
to hop (on) a babe
to hump
to jump (on)
someone's bones
to kick it
to kick it around
to knock boots
to knock off a piece
to lap dance
to lay

to lay some pipe
to lie together
to lock boots
to make feet for
children's shoes
to make it
to make love to
to make love with
to make some noise
to make the beast
with two backs
to mate with
to meld
to melt
to nail P
to get a piece of trim

to oil the notch
to partake of the flesh
to play hanky-panky
to play rub-belly
to play the Adam and Eve game
to plook
to polish one's ass on the top sheet
to pop
to pop it in
to pork
to pump
to reach third base
to ride a St. George
to ride pussy
to ride the bitch's seat
to rock someone's world
to rock the spot
to roger
to romp
to rub the stubble
to screw
to serve
to set one's post
to shag

to sleep together
to sleep with
to slip (someone) the meat
to spoon
to stoke
to stroke
to swive
to swive with
to take a turn
to take Nebuchadnezzar
  out to grass
to thrimble
to throw the"D"
to throw the"P"
to throw the dagger
to thump
to trim
to twang
to wax
to wax some ass
to wear it out
to whip the"Y"
to wiggle one's bean
to womp on someone
to worship at the pink altar

Oral Sex

Cunnilingus:

Carpet munching
Gamahuche
Minette

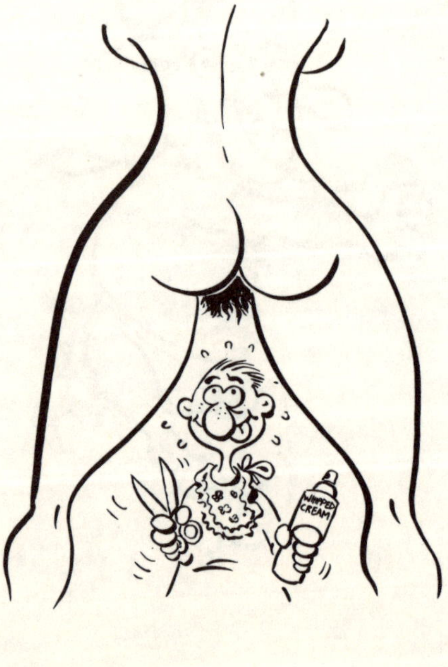

Muff diving
Muff noshing
Rug munching
to do or give a hum job
to eat (someone)
to eat at the"Y"
to eat out
to eat pussy
to gamahuche
to give face
to give head
to go down on
to sniff in the can
to suck off
to talk to the
canoe driver
to worship at
the shrine of love
to yodel in the canyon

Fellatio:

A blow job
A knob job
Knob gobbling
to do or give a hum job
to eat tube steak
to fellate
to give face
to give head
to give skull
to go down on
to play the bagpipe
to play the skin flute
to slob the knob
to slobber on the throbber
to suck
to suck cock
to suck off

Mutual:

69
Soixante-neuf
Tête-bêche

Condom

Capot anglais
French letter
French tickler
Frogskin
Jim hat
Jimmy hat
Jo-bag
(Rubber) Johnny
Noddy
Raincoat
Rubber
Scumbag
Sheath
Skin

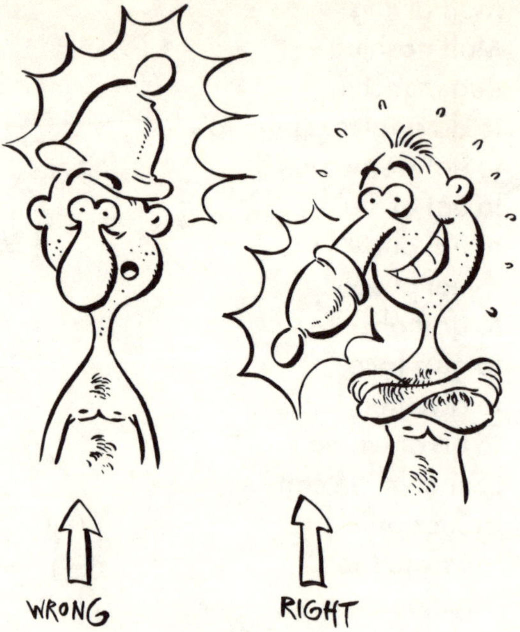

Orgasm

The acme of pleasure
The big"O"
The crisis of pleasure
to bring down one's love
to bring down one's spend
to bust a nut
to climax
to come
to cream one's jeans
to cream one's panties
to cum
to dissolve oneself
to get off
to get one's cookies off
to get one's nuts off
to get one's rocks off
to give down the
  liquor of love
to let down the milk
to make someone scream
to obtain an emission
to open the floodgates
  of love's reservoir
to pay down one's tribute
to pop off
to pop one's cookies

to pop one's cork
to pop one's nuts
to shoot one's load
to shoot one's roe
to shoot one's wad
to spend
to spew
to spill one's liquor
to spunk (someone) up

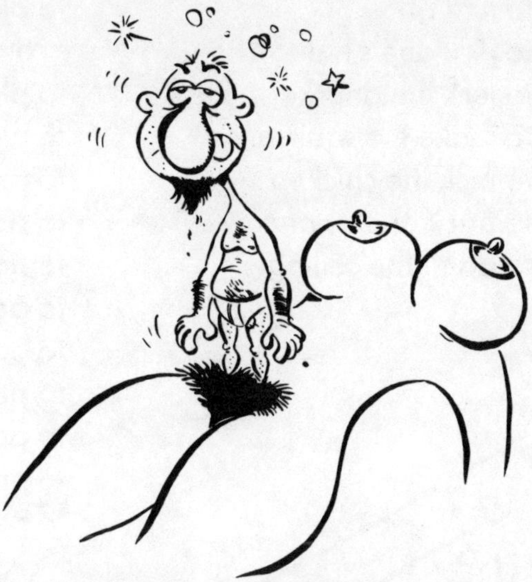

Masturbation

Male

A hand job
A one-stick drum
  improvisation
Onan's Olympics
The Portuguese pump
to bang the bishop
to bash the bishop
to be slakin' the bacon
to beat off
to beat one's dummy
to beat one's log
to beat one's meat
to beat the bishop
to beat the hog
to bring (oneself) off
to burp the worm
to choke one's chicken
to choke the gopher
to crank one's shank
to cuff one's meat
to do a doodle-dandler
to file one's fun-rod
to fist fuck
to fist one's mister
to flex one's sex
to flog one's dog
to flog the bishop
to flog the dolphin
to flong one's dong
to frig oneself
to gallop one's antelope
to get (oneself) off
to grease one's pipe
to hand-jive
to hone the bone
to hump one's hose

to jerk off
to jerk one's mutton
to jerk the gherkin
to make the squirrel spit
to milk the chicken
to pack one's palm
to paint the ceiling

to play a flute solo
  on one's meat whistle
to play the male organ
to play with oneself
to please one's pisser
to point one's social finger
to polish one's sword
to pound one's peenie
to pound one's pud
to pound the flounder
to prompt the porpoise
to prune the fifth limb
to pull one's pud

to pull one's taffy
to pull one's wire
to pull oneself off
to pull the Pope
to pump one's pickle
to rub off
to run one's hand
up the flagpole
to screw off
to shake hands with
the unemployed
to sharpen one's pencil
to shine one's pole
to shoot the tadpoles
to slam one's hammer
to slam one's Spam
to slap one's wrapper
to spank the monkey
to spank the salami
to strike the pink match
to stroke off
to stroke one's poker
to stroke the dog
to talk with Rosy Palm
and her five sisters
to thump one's pumper
to tickle one's pickle
to toss oneself off
to tweak one's twinkie
to unclog the pipes
to varnish one's pole
to walk the dog
to wank off
to watch the eyelid movies
to wax one's dolphin
to whack off
to whip one's dripper
to wonk one's conker
to yang one's wang
to yank off
to yank one's crank
to yank the yam

Female

to beat the beaver
to bring (oneself) off
to buttonhole
to clap one's clit
to cook cucumbers
to finger-fuck
to finger oneself
to frig oneself
to get (oneself) off
to grease the gash
to hide the hotdog
to hit the slit
to hose the hole
to juice one's sluice
to make waves
to pet the poodle
to play stinkfinger
to play with oneself
to rub off
to screw off
to slam the clam
to stroke off

Chapter 2: More parts of speech

Grammar and shit

Nouns
Hauptwörter

Singular – plural
Einzahl – Mehrzahl

tit	tits
bone	bones
box	boxes
snatch	snatches

- Bei den meisten Hauptwörtern (nouns) wird die Mehrzahl (plural) durch Anhängen von *-s* / *-es* gebildet.

mouse	mice
foot	feet
man	men
woman	women

- Diese Hauptwörter haben **besondere Mehrzahlformen.**

- I need a *piece* of ass.
- How many *pieces* do you want?
- I think one *piece* is enough.

- Wenn von einem oder mehreren einzelnen Stücken die Rede ist, verwendet man *piece(s)* of:

snatch	– a piece of snatch
nookie	– one piece of nookie
hair-pie	– two pieces of hair-pie

- Do you like bald *poontang*?
- No, I like a lot of *hair* on it.

The class was a bunch of *bullshit*. *It's* always a bunch of *bullshit*.

- Man verwendet Hauptwörter wie z.B. *nookie* und *poontang* **nur** in der **Einzahl** (wie auch *pud, meat, bullshit* usw.)

The "fucking" genitive

Der *fucking* Genitiv

- Whose fucking cat is shitting on the sofa?
- I think it's Mr. Catherall's fucking cat.

- Whose fucking books are these?
- I think they're Patrick's fucking books.

- Can you show me your fucking apartment?
- Sure. This is the fucking living-room, here's my fucking parents' bedroom and over there's my fucking brother's room.

- Bei Personen wird im **Genetiv** der **Singular** mit *-'s* und der **Plural** mit *-s'* gebildet.

– Since her husband died, Mrs. Jones gets her bangers *from the butcher's.*
– She also likes to get her buns *at the baker's.*
– Perhaps she will buy a toy *at Dr. Miller's?*
– No, she prefers to get her greens *at the supermarket.*

- Wenn von **Geschäften** die Rede ist, verwendet man die Berufsbezeichnung oder den Namen mit *-'s* (*baker's, Dr. Miller's*).
  Man verwendet den Genetiv auch bei Ausdrücken wie *at the doctor's*.
  Man sagt aber *at the supermarket*.

– What's the *name of your dong?*
– Mr. Happy.

- Bei **Sachen** verwendet man keinen Genetiv, sondern einen Ausdruck mit *of. . . : the name of your dong.*

– I want *a bottle of tequila,* a *packet of condoms,* and two *six-packs of beer.*

- Nach Namen für **Behälter** wie *bottle, can, box, cup, glass, six-pack* benennt man den Inhalt immer durch einen Ausdruck mit *of... : a cup of coffee*.

Adjectives and adverbs
Eigenschaftswörter und
Umstandswörter

Adjectives
Eigenschaftswörter

Comparative and superlative forms of adjectives
Steigerungsformen der Eigenschaftswörter

- I'll get some French ticklers from the sex shop.
- Why don't you buy them at the drug store? They're *cheaper* there.
- I think you can get them *cheapest* at the supermarket.
- But why are they *more expensive* at the sex shop?
- Well, the babes who work there are the *best* and *most beautiful* in town. They're not like the sleazebags at the drugstore.
- Well, I think it's *better* to check out the fuck-bunnies before you buy, don't you?

Es gibt zwei verschiedene Steigerungsformen: Formen auf *-er* und *-est* und Formen mit *more* und *most*.

		comparative form	**superlative form**
einsilbige Adjektive	dumb hot	dumber hotter	dumbest hottest
zweisilbige Adjektive auf -y und -er	shitty sheer	shittier sheerer	shittiest sheerest
andere mehrsilbige Adjektive	fucked-up humongous	more fucked-up more humongous	most fucked-up most humongous
besondere Form	good	better	best

– Who's the dumbest motherfucker in our class?
– Joe is.
– No, I think Tom is dumber *than* Joe.
– Oh no. Tom isn't *as* dumb *as* Joe. Joe is *as* dumb *as* a barrel of hair.

- Wenn man sagen will, daß Personen oder Sachen (nicht) so groß, gut, interessant usw. sind wie andere, verwendet man *(not) as . . . as*.

- Wenn man sagen will, daß Personen oder Sachen größer, besser, interessanter usw. sind als andere, verwendet man *. . . than*.

Adverbs
Umstandswörter

-ly adverbs
Umstandswörter mit -ly

- Please be *careful.*
- I always do it *carefully*. I never do the deadly deed*.

- The sheep were *lucky*.
- *Luckily* the shepherd was arrested.

- Bob is a *slow* motherfucker.
- I bet he even farts *slowly*.

- You must be *quiet* in the bedroom.
- I always come *quietly.*

*ungeschützter GV

- *careful, lucky, slow, quiet* sind **Eigenschaftswörter** (*adjectives*). Sie beschreiben, welche **Eigenschaften** Personen, Tiere oder Sachen haben.

- *carefully, luckily, slowly, quietly* sind **Umstandswörter** *(adverbs).* Sie werden *-ly adverbs* genannt, weil sie durch Anhängen von *-ly* an das Eigenschaftswort gebildet werden.
  Umstandswörter geben an, **wie** (auf welche Weise) **etwas geschieht** (geschah, geschehen soll usw.).

Good – Well

– Souza is sure a fine motherfucker, isn't she?
– Oh yes, she sure looks *good*. She couldn't look *better*.

Are you doing *well* in English?
Fucking right, it couldn't fucking be *better*.

- *good* ist ein Eigenschaftswort, das Umstandswort heißt *well*. Die Steigerungsform von *well* heißt *better* (wie die Steigerungsform von *good*).

The articles
Die Artikel
(Geschlechtswörter – aber nicht was ihr denkt!)

The definite article
Der bestimmte Artikel

The

the bald-headed candidate
the crack of doom

- Im Gegensatz zum Deutschen, gibt es im Englischen nur einen bestimmten Artikel. *The* wird immer verwendet, ganz gleich ob das Hauptwort männlich, weiblich oder sächlich ist.

There are no cute boys *at school.*
I hate going *to bed* with a hard-on.

- Achtung: In Ortsangaben wie *at school, to bed* verwendet man keinen Artikel.

The indefinite article

Der unbestimmte Artikel

a, an

a love-pillow – *an* orb

- Vor Mitlauten (*consonants*) verwendet man: **a.**
  Vor Selbstlauten (*vowels*) verwendet man: **an.**

He is *a* bastard by birth, but *an* asshole by choice.

- Wenn man angibt, welche Tätigkeit jemand ausübt, verwendet man *a bzw. an* vor der Tätigkeit: *he is a bastard, she is an asshole*.

– Do you know the answer to the next question?
– Sorry, I *haven't got a fucking* clue.
– You're *no fucking* Einstein, are you?.

- Wenn man sagen will, daß etwas nicht da ist, oder daß man es nicht hat, verwendet man meist *not . . . a fucking* anstelle von *no fucking*.

Pronouns
Pronomen (Fürwörter)

Personal Pronouns
Personalpronomen (persönliche Fürwörter)

subject	other parts
I	saw a monstrous wang in front of *me*.
She	asked Jim to tie *her* up.

- Es gibt **zwei Formen der persönlichen Fürwörter:** eine für den Satzgegenstand (subject) und eine für die anderen Satzteile (other parts).

singular		plural	
subject	**other parts**	**subject**	**other parts**
I	me	we	us
you	you	you	you
he	him		
she	her	they	them
it	it		

the girl → she / her the boy → he / him the table, the lamp, the bed → it / it the dog → it / it	the girls, the boys, the things → they / them

Spot is a good dog. *He* always tries to hump my leg. I like *him*.

- Für **Personen** sagt man **he / she (him / her),** für **Sachen** sagt man **it.** In der **Mehrzahl** heißt es für Personen und Sachen **they (them).** Für **Tiere** verwendet man **it**, wenn die Tiere aber einen Namen haben sagt man meist *he / she (him / her).*

Possessive Pronouns

Possessivpronomen (Besitzanzeigende Fürwörter)

singular		plural	
my your his her its	name / names	our your their	name / names

Relative Pronouns

Bezügliche Fürwörter

I like *boys*	*who / that* wear girl's underwear.
Sandra doesn't like a *boy*	*who / that* is a wimp.
I like *animals*	*that* are woolly and fat.
Have you got a *poster*	*that* shows sheep?

- Für **Personen** (Einzahl und Mehrzahl) verwendet man *who* oder *that*.
  Für **Sachen** (Einzahl und Mehrzahl) verwendet man *that*.
  Für **Tiere** (Einzahl und Mehrzahl) verwendet man meist *that*.

Other Pronouns

Andere Fürwörter

some

– I've got some beer.
– And I've got *some* smokes.
– Great. Let's have *some.*

– Can I have *some* seafood, please?
– Of course. How about *some* bearded clam?

- Man verwendet *some* vor Hauptwörtern in der Mehrzahl (als Mehrzahlform von *a: a smoke – some smokes*).

- Man verwendet *some* anstelle von Hauptwörtern: *lend me some (smokes).*

any

- Are you trying to give me some shit?.
- No, I'm not trying to give you *any* shit.
- Are you just passing out some wolf tickets?
- No, I'm not passing out *any* wolf tickets either.

- Nach **not** verwendet man **any** (anstelle von some).

some – any in der Frage

- Can I have some fur-pie?
- Sorry, I've got very little and I need it.

- Did your parents have any children that lived?
- What do you mean? The best part of you ran down your mother's leg.

- In der ersten Frage verwendet man *some*, weil man **um etwas bittet** (und annimmt, daß man es bekommen könnte).
- In der zweiten Frage verwendet man *any*, weil man **nach etwas fragt** (was man nicht weiß).

some- und any-Wörter

- *Somebody* cut the cheese.
- It smells like someone died.
- Did *anybody* hear anything?.
- The smeller is the feller.

- Tell me *something* about sheep.
- Sorry, I don't know *anything* about them.

- *Somebody, something, anybody, anything* sind "some- und any-Wörter". Man verwendet sie so, wie man *some* und *any* verwendet.

much, many – a lot, lots

– Billy doesn't feel well. He has eaten *too much pussy*. – Well, you shouldn't give him *so much*. – *How many frogskins* do you have left? – *Not* very *many*. – And *how many* do you have? – Oh, *lots*. – How is Jane? – Oh, she's quite nice, but she doesn't put out *a lot*. The boys and girls are having *lots of* fun.

- Man verwendet *much / many* mit oder anstelle von Hauptwörtern in der **Einzahl** oder in der **Mehrzahl**.

- Man verwendet *much* und *many* meist in **Fragen** (*how much / many*) und **nach not, so,** und **too** (*not much, too many usw.*).

- In anderen Sätzen verwendet man eher *a lot of ...* oder *lots of ...* **vor Hauptwörtern** oder *a lot* oder *lots* **anstelle von Hauptwörtern**.

one, ones

- What do you want for your birthday, Nadine?
- A pearl necklace.
- But I just gave you *one*.
- Yes, but I want *another one*.

- How do you like those knockers?
- They're nice. But what about the *ones* over there?

- I like these sheep, don't you?
- Yes, but I think *the black ones* are better.

- Man verwendet *one / ones* mit oder anstelle von Hauptwörtern in der **Einzahl** oder in der **Mehrzahl**.
- Menn man **nach einem Eigenschaftswort** ein Hauptwort nicht wiederholen will, verwendet man *one* oder *ones*:
  a pearl necklace – another one
  sheep – the black ones

Fragewörter mit *fuck*

Why the fuck	are you learning English?
When the fuck	are you going to get it right?
Where the fuck	do you live?
How the fuck	do I get there?

- *Why, when, where,* und *how* in Verbindung mit einem Verb werden mit *the fuck* ergänzt.

What the fuck	did you do last night?
What the fuck	shall we do now?

- *What* auf eine Tätigkeit bezogen wird mit *the fuck* ergänzt.

Who the fuck	is Alice?

- *Who* + sein (to be) wird mit *the fuck* ergänzt.

Who the fuck / fucking	cares?

- *Who* + andere Verben kann entweder mit *the fuck* oder *fucking* ergänzt werden.

Which fucking	one do you want, the one that tastes like strawberry or the one that tastes like banana?
Which fucking	comes first, the subject or the verb?

- *Which* wird benutzt wenn eine Entscheidung zwischen mehreren Möglichkeiten getroffen werden muß und wird mit *fucking* ergänzt.

What fucking	*time* is it?
Which fucking	*way* is the train station?
Whose fucking	*dog* is this?

- *What, which,* und *whose auf ein Substantiv bezogen werden mit fucking* ergänzt.

How fucking	*much* time do you need?
	old are you?
	much money have you got?
	many books have you got?

- *How* in Verbindung mit einem Adjektiv oder Adverb, z.B. *much, old,* und *many,* wird mit *fucking* ergänzt.

Chapter 3
The Sentence

As we have seen, the girls have their parts, and the boys have their parts. Now it's time to put those parts together –

The parts of the sentence & word order

Satzteile und Wortfolge

subject	verb link	other parts	
Harry	beat	the bishop.	(object)
Susan	had	a shit fit.	(object)
My sister	bought	a C.F.M.* T-shirt.	(object)
The weenie-wagger	flashes	at night.	(adverb of time)
Bulldykes	eat	at the"Y".	(adverb of place)

*come fuck me

- In diesen Sätzen ist die **Wortfolge:**
  Satzgegenstand (subject) **Prädikat** (verb link) **weitere Satzteile** (other parts)

- **Nach dem Prädikat** (verb link) können folgen:
  Ergänzungen (objects)

The place of the adverbs in the sentence

Die Stellung der Umstandsbestimmungen im Satz

Adverbs of place and adverbs of time at the beginning of the sentence

Orts- und Zeitbestimmungen am Anfang des Satzes

adverbs	subject	verb link	other parts
In the morning	I	had	a rod on.
Then	I	had	a nooner.
At work	it	was	a bitch.

- Orts- oder Zeitbestimmungen können am Anfang des Satzes stehen. **Nach einer Orts- oder Zeitbestimmung** am Anfang des Satzes ist die **Wortfolge:**

Satzgegenstand (subject) **Prädikat** (verb link) **weitere Satzteile** (other parts)

Adverbs of place and adverbs of time at the end of the sentence

Orts- und Zeitbestimmungen am Ende des Satzes

subject	verb link	adverbs of place	adverbs of time
John	stayed	at the sheep farm	last year.
Susan	sat	on my face	after school.
I	worshipped	at the pink altar	before supper.

Am Ende des Satzes stehen die
Ortsbestimmungen vor den **Zeitbestimmungen.**
(adverbs of place) (adverbs of time)

Adverbs in the middle of the sentence

Umstandswörter in der Mitte des Satzes

subject	**adverb**	**verb**	
Mr. Hardwick	usually	buys	a few things at the sex shop.
He	often	sees	Mrs. Smythe there
and (he)	sometimes	rubs	the stubble with her.
But he	never	stays	for tea.

- Die **Umstandswörter** (adverbs) stehen in diesen Sätzen **vor dem Verb.**

Questions

Fragesätze

question word	**auxiliary**	**subject**	**verb**	**other parts**
	Can't	you	drive	a fucking car?
	Is	Grace	slamming	her clam?
	Have	you	got	a banana in your pants?
	Did	you	step	on a duck?
Where	has	Patrick	put	my fucking book?
When	will	they	come	back from the movie?
How long	does	Mike	have to stay	in jail?
Who	did	you	bone	at the party?

- Die ersten vier Fragen sind **Entscheidungsfragen** (*yes/no questions*): man kann sie mit *yes* oder *no* beantworten.

- Die anderen Fragen sind **Wortfragen** (*word questions*): sie beginnen mit einem Fragewort (*question word).*

- In allen diesen Fragen ist die **Wortfolge:**

Fragewort	**Hilfsverb**	**Satzgegenstand**	**Verb**
(question word)	(auxiliary)	(subject)	(verb)

- Wenn kein anderes Hilfsverb im Satz ist, verwendet man *do, does, did.*

> Grace plays the bagpipes.
> Does Barbara play the bagpipes, too?
>
> Mike broke his pencil.
> Did he sharpen it too fast?

- In diesen Fragen erscheint die *-s* form: *does* und die Vergangenheitsform: *did* nur beim Hilfsverb. Das Verb steht in der Grundform: *play, sharpen*.

subject	**verb link**	**other parts**
What	happens	if you fail the exam?
(You	are	S.O.L.*)
Who	took	my blow-up doll?
(Henry	took	it.)
Who	wants	a quickie?
(I	suggest	you go fuck yourself.)

* shit out of luck

- In diesen Sätzen ist das **Fragewort** (question word: *what* und *who*) **Satzgegenstand** (*subject*).
  Die **Wortfolge** ist hier wie im Aussagesatz:
  Satzgegenstand (subject) **Prädikat** (verb link) **weitere Satzteile** (other parts)

  Man verwendet **nicht** *do, does, did.*

Negative sentences
Verneinung

subject	**verb link**		**other parts**
	auxiliary + not	**verb**	
I	can't	remember	shit.
A trouser snake	will not	be	tamed.
You	shouldn't	get	your balls in an uproar.
Sorry, I	won't	have	time for a quickie.
A hard dick	doesn't	have	a conscience.
I	don't	think	he is a faggot.
She	did not	give	a rat's ass.

- Das Wörtchen *not* steht immer nach einem Hilfsverb (auxiliary).
- Wenn kein anderes Hilfsverb im Satz ist, verwendet man *do, does, did.*
- Bei der **Verneinung** verwendet man oft **Kurzformen** wie:
  can't, won't, shouldn't.

Short sentences in dialogues
Kurzsätze in Dialogen

Short answers
Kurzantworten

– Are you a German?
– No, I'm not. Do I fucking look like one?

– Is Michèle a bimbo?
– Yes, she is. / No, she isn't.

– Do you like ice-cream?
– No, I don't. Why? Are you writing a fucking book?

- Nach *yes* und *no* verwendet man häufig **Kurzantworten**. Das ist höflicher als bloß *yes* oder *no* zu sagen.

- Statt *yes* und *no* kann man in Kurzantworten aber auch andere Wendungen gebrauchen, z. B.

– Can you help me, please?
– Fuck off and die.

– Do you like a girl with a big bohunkus?
– Does a bear shit in the woods?

– Do you like ice-cream?
– Is the Pope Catholic?

– What time is it?
– Time to buy a watch.

Short questions at the end of a sentence

Angehängte Kurzfragen

– I'm as horny as a hootowl, *aren't you?*
– Yes. But the girls here are all butt-ugly, *aren't they?*
– I guess we're just shit out of luck, *aren't we?*

– Mike sure stepped on his wankus, *didn't he?*
– Yes, he really fucked-up.

– You weren't choking your chicken, *were you?*
– No. Of course not.

– You didn't see anything, *did you?*
– No. Of course not.

- Wenn man wissen will, was jemand von dem, was man sagt, hält, kann man an seine Aussage eine **Kurzfrage** anhängen.

- Kurzfragen bestehen immer aus einem **Hilfsverb** (*are, do* usw.) und einem **Fürwort** (*they, you* usw.).

- Nach bejahten Aussagen verwendet man eine verneinte Kurzfrage:

+	–
I'm as horny as a hootowl,	*aren't you?*

- Nach verneinten Aussagen verwendet man eine bejahte Kurzfrage:

–	+
You *weren't* choking your chicken,	*were you?*

- Wenn in der bejahten Aussage kein Hilfsverb ist, verwendet man in der Kurzfrage *don't, doesn't* oder *didn't*:

+	–
Mike sure stepped on his wankus,	*didn't he?*

Relative clauses

Relativsätze

	Relative clause
He likes boys	who / that are rude and rough with him.
He'd also like to have an animal	that is rude and rough with him.
Sandra likes boys	who like whips and chains.
Do you have any condoms	that have knobs on them?

- Die Nebensätze auf der rechten Seite sind **Relativsätze** (relative clauses). Sie sagen etwas über das vorangehende Hauptwort (noun) aus:
  Welche Jungen? – Was für ein Tier?

Chapter 4: The Tenses

The simple present

Das *simple present*

Man bildet das *simple present* wie folgt:

Simple present		
I	diddle	grope
you	diddle	grope
he / she / it	diddles	gropes
we	diddle	grope
you	diddle	grope
they	diddle	grope

Exercise 4.1

Übung 4.1

Schreibe die Form der folgenden Verben im *simple present* auf:

1.	Tom always ____ (get) a hard-on when he ____ (read) stroke-books.
2.	School ________ (suck) so bad it ________ (make) me want to puke.
3.	Every time he ____ (ask) her for a date, she ____ (give) him the finger.

Exercise 4.2

Übung 4.2

Irgend jemand hat sich einen Scherz erlaubt und die Verben aus dieser Geschichte geklaut. Dr. McNaughety fand aber das Versteck (eingeklemmt zwischen Pornos und illegalen Substanzen – ihr wißt, wer ihr seid!) Also setzt sie gefälligst wieder ein, ihr kleinen Scheißer!

teases	milks
wears	looks
is	watches
pets	screw

Joe ___________harmless, but he would ___________a snake if someone would hold its mouth open. Most of the time, however, he just ___________ his chicken while he ___________ the eyelid movies.

Jane ___________ quite different. She ___________ slutty clothes and ___________ the boys, but she never admits that she ___________ the poodle.

The present progressive

Das *present progressive*

Man bildet das *present progressive* wie folgt:

Present progressive		
	bejaht **Langform / Kurzform**	**verneint** **Langform / Kurzform**
I	am bonin' / I'm bonin'	am not bonin' / I'm not bonin'
you	are bonin' / you're bonin'	are not bonin' / you're not bonin'
he / she / it	is bonin' / 's bonin'	is not bonin' / 's not bonin'
we	are bonin' / we're bonin'	are not bonin' / we're not bonin'
you	are bonin' / you're bonin'	are not bonin' / you're not bonin'
they	are bonin' / they're bonin'	are not bonin' / they're not bonin'

Exercise 4.3

Übung 4.3

Unser Zeichner macht gerade eine dunkle Phase durch.
Kannst du trotzdem erkennen, was auf den Bildern zu sehen ist bzw. was die Leute machen und womit?
Die Anfangsbuchstaben bilden den Namen einer Berühmtheit.
Wer ist es?

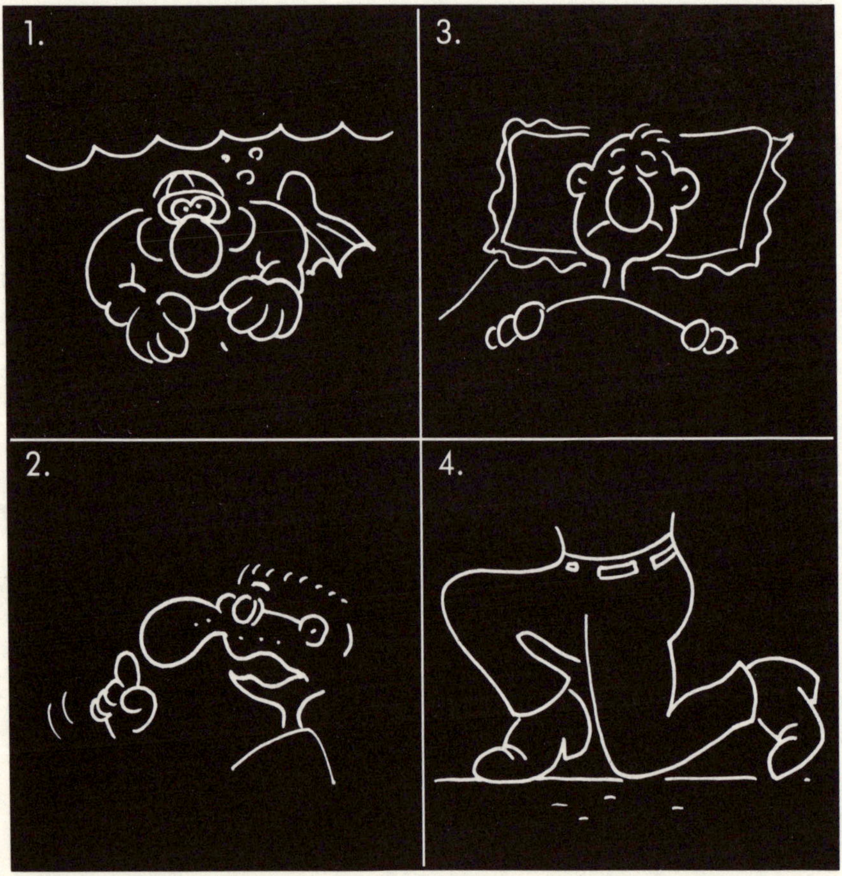

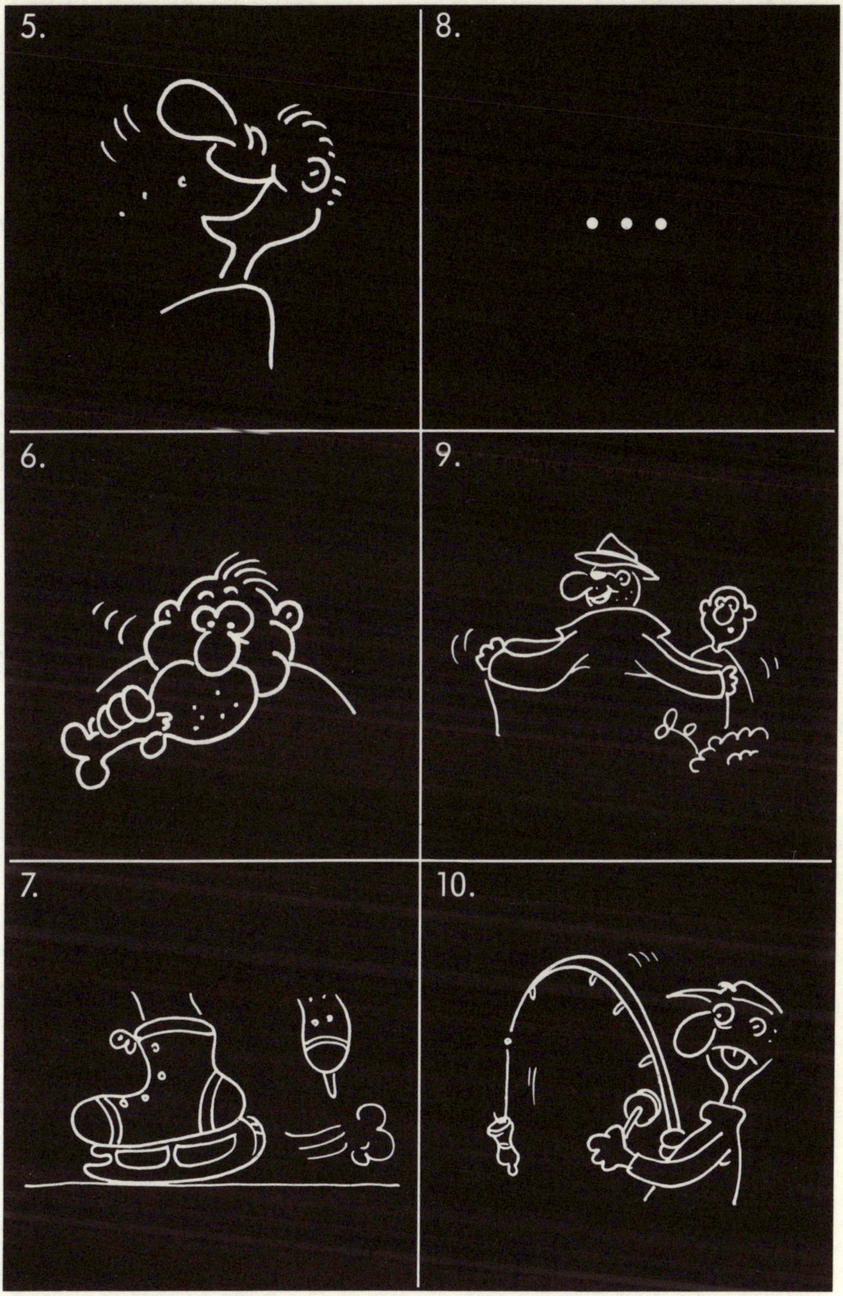
5.
8.
6.
9.
7.
10.

11.
14.
12.
15.
13.
16.

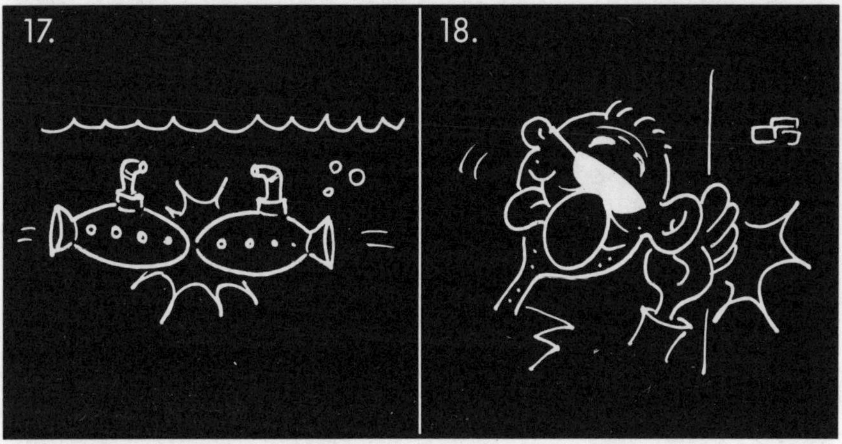

The name of the famous person is ____________________

The simple past

Das *simple past*

Bei der Bildung des *simple past* muß man zwischen den **regelmäßigen** und den **unregelmäßigen** Verben unterscheiden.

- Bei den **regelmäßigen Verben** hängt man ein *-ed* an den Infinitiv an und zwar bei allen Personen, zum Beispiel:

screw	screwed
roger	rogered
play the skin flute	played the skin flute

- Die unregelmäßigen Verben dagegen haben eine eigene Form, die man einfach auswendig lernen muß, zum Beispiel:

do a bottom wetter	did a bottom wetter
get laid	got laid
go tummy tickling	went tummy tickling
hide the salami	hid the salami
eat	ate

- Ganz so einfach mit dem Anhängen von *-ed* ist es allerdings nicht. Es gibt bestimmte Schreibregeln, die man beachten muß:

- Ein stummes *-e* fällt weg:

diddle	diddled
fettle	fettled
fumble	fumbled

- Das *-y* nach einem Konsonanten wird zum *-i:*

monkey	monkied

- Manche Konsonanten verdoppeln sich nach einem einfachen Vokal:

whip the dripper	whipped the dripper
pull the Pope	pulled the Pope
flog the dolphin	flogged the dolphin

Exercise 4.4

Übung 4.4

Vervollständige die Sätze mit der *simple past*-Form der Verben:

1. Who __________ up my Walkman? (screw)
2. On Saturday, I __________ muff diving. (go)
3. Every night he __________ the worm. (burp)

4. First they __________ for awhile, then she __________ his pickle. (fumble / tickle)

5. The exam __________ a real mind-fucker. (is)

The past progressive

Das *past progressive*

Das *past progressive* wird mit *was / were* + der *-ing* Form des Vollverbs gebildet:

	bejaht **Langform**	**verneint** **Langform / Kurzform**
I	was honing	was not / wasn't honing
You	were yanking	were / weren't yanking
He / She / It	was pulling	was / wasn't pulling
We	were varnishing	were / weren't varnishing
You	were whipping	were / weren't whipping
They	were humping	were / weren't humping

Exercise 4.5

Übung 4.5

Als Dr. McNaughety die Hausaufgaben einsammeln wollte, hatten alle eine Ausrede parat. Was kam wirklich dazwischen?

1. read

3. swim

2. buy

4. watch

5. catch

6. stay

1. Johnny ______________________________ comics.

2. Jane ___________________________ some new CDs.

3. Sammy __________________________________ .

4. Rhonda _________________________________ TV.

5. Robert _____________________________ some Z's.

6. Kevin ____________________________ home alone.

The present perfect
Das *present perfect*

- Im Englischen wird das *present perfect* immer mit *have / has* + Partizip (3. Form) gebildet. Im Deutschen dagegen mit "haben" oder "sein". Im Englischen sieht das *present perfect* also wie folgt aus:

	bejaht **Langform / Kurzform**	**verneint** **Langform / Kurzform**
I	have / 've tweaked	have not / haven't tweaked
You	have / 've plooked	have not / haven't plooked
He / She / It	has / 's pleased	has not / hasn't pleased
We	have / 've stroked	have not / haven't stroked
You	have / 've waxed	have not / haven't waxed
They	have / 've hosed	have not / haven't hosed

- Bei **regelmäßigen Verben** wird das Partizip aus dem Infinitiv + *-ed* gebildet. Es ist die gleiche Form wie die des *simple past,* zum Beispiel:
  enjoy + –ed → enjoyed

Exercise 4.6
Übung 4.6

A lettersquare

Die 3. Form (Partizip) der 15 unten aufgelisteten Verben hat Dr. McNaughety in dem Lettersquare versteckt. 5 davon sind normal (→), 2 von rechts nach links (←), 5 von oben nach unten (↓), und 3 von unten nach oben (↑) geschrieben.

Die Verben im Infinitiv:

dork – feel – grease – hose – hump – muff dive – please – prompt – rub – shag – shoot – strike – unclog – varnish – yank

Y	E	J	W	Y	R	J	H	K	X	A	I	D	Z	T
A	H	V	B	D	Q	O	U	C	P	W	S	D	R	A
N	S	K	F	O	K	-	M	U	I	L	E	K	H	M
K	M	R	-	R	U	H	P	R	O	M	P	T	E	D
E	O	M	T	K	V	U	E	T	Q	W	C	X	L	X
D	E	U	T	E	E	P	D	S	H	A	G	G	E	D
U	Z	N	L	D	P	X	A	D	I	Q	F	Q	J	C
B	N	C	Y	Y	D	E	V	I	D	-	F	F	U	M
N	P	L	E	A	S	E	D	-	G	D	P	T	B	A
D	F	O	Z	S	N	V	A	R	N	I	S	H	E	D
E	U	G	R	E	A	S	E	D	J	H	D	Y	B	O
B	M	G	S	B	V	O	J	L	A	C	G	T	O	S
B	T	E	E	-	K	P	M	L	K	V	P	L	C	H
U	G	D	U	H	R	D	E	S	O	H	G	E	W	O
R	F	S	Y	I	F	Q	N	C	G	N	R	F	Z	T

ZZZ !!! Na, ah, schon fertig? Ah, dann wollen wir zum nächsten Thema kommen, nämlich zum, ah, oh yes, zum ...

The going to and will future

Das *going to-* und *will-future*

- Das *going to future* wird wie folgt gebildet:

Subjekt	be	going to	Infinitiv	andere Satzteile
I	am	going to	take	a whiz.
He	is	going to	buy	a blow-up doll.
We	are	going to	piss off	our teacher.

- Man benutzt das *going to future,* wenn man über zukünftige Pläne und Vorhaben sprechen möchte.

Exercise 4.7

Übung 4.7

Das Wochende steht vor der Tür! Was haben diese Leute am Wochenende vor?

1. Jerry	2. Mr. Jones

.... tweak	.... yodel

3. Gwendoline	4. Dave

.... unpack	.... hang-out

1. Jerry ______________________________ his twinkie.

2. Mr. Jones ____________________________ in the canyon.

3. Gwendoline ____________________ her whips and chains.

4. Dave ________________________________ at the disco.

The will future

Das *will-future*

- Das *will-future* wird wie folgt gebildet:

	bejaht **Lang- / Kurzform**	**verneint** **Lang- / Kurzform**
I	will / 'll see	will not / won't see
You	will / 'll see	will not / won't see
He / She / It	will / 'll see	will not / won't see
We	will / 'll see	will not / won't see
You	will / 'll see	will not / won't see
They	will / 'll see	will not / won't see

- Man benutzt das *will-future*, um über zukünftige Vorgänge, auf die wir keinen Einfluß haben, zu sprechen.

- Man benutzt das *will-future* auch, um eine Vorhersage zu machen oder eine Vermutung zu äußern.

Exercise 4.8

Übung 4.8

Setze die angegebenen Verben ein.
Benutze dabei nur das *will-future*, und zwar in der Langform.

1. If that two-bagger touches me, I think I ______________ (upchuck).

2. You had better take a shower. Otherwise you __________ (get) a case of the crabs.

3. As Robinson Crusoe said to his wife: "If you're not down Thursday, I ______________________ (be) up Friday".

4. If we miss the last train, we ______________________ (be) shit out of luck.

5. If you don't stop, I ______________ (cream) my panties.

6. We _______ (be) fucked if we fail the test. We must study.

Solutions to exercises

Exercise 4.1

1. gets / reads
2. sucks / makes
3. asks / gives

Exercise 4.2

The correct order is:

looks
screw
milks
watches
is
wears
teases
pets

Exercise 4.3

1. (diving)

2. (arguing)

3. (sleeping)

4. (kneeling)

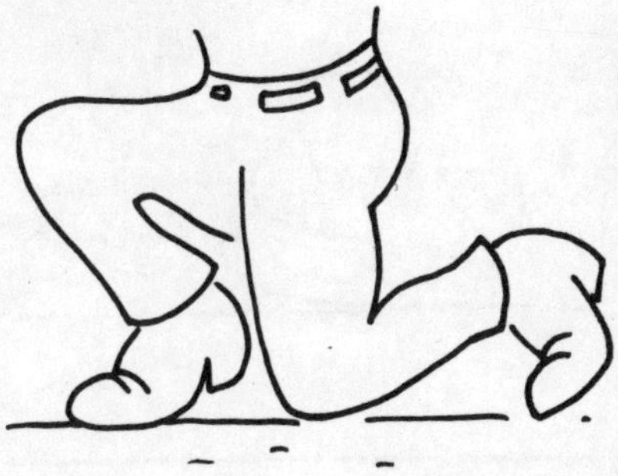

5. (laughing)

6. (eating)

7. (ice skating)

8. (nothing)

• • •

9. (exposing himself)

10. (angling)

11. (raining)

12. (studying)

13. (celebrating)

14. (hammering)

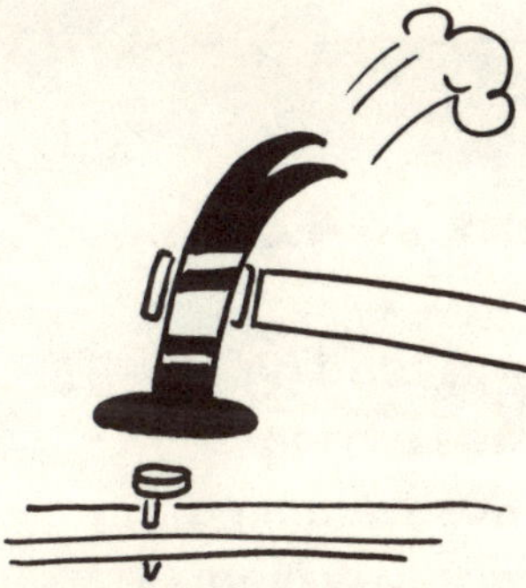

15. (locking)

16. (orbiting)

17. (crashing)

18. (hearing)

The name of the famous person is **das kleine Arschloch**

Exercise 4.4

1. screwed
2. went
3. burped
4. fumbled / tickled
5. was

Exercise 4.5

1. was reading
2. was buying
3. was swimming
4. was watching
5. was catching
6. was staying

Exercise 4.6

Lettersquare

Y							H	K						
A				D			U	C						
N				O			M	U						
K				R			P	R	O	M	P	T	E	D
E				K			E	T						
D		U		E			D	S	H	A	G	G	E	D
		N		D										
		C			D	E	V	I	D	-	F	F	U	M
	P	L	E	A	S	E	D							
D		O				V	A	R	N	I	S	H	E	D
E		G	R	E	A	S	E	D						
B		G										T		S
B		E										L		H
U		D				D	E	S	O	H		E		O
R												F		T

Exercise 4.7

1. is going to tweak
2. is going to yodel.
3. is going to unpack
4. is going to hang-out

Exercise 4.8

1. will upchuck
2. will get
3. will be
4. will be
5. will cream
6. will be

Glossary

Glossar

Babe (Substantiv): eine gutaussehende junge Frau

Bimbo (Substantiv): 1. ein Dummchen; 2. eine Niete (unabhängig vom Geschlecht)

Bitch (Substantiv): 1. Biest oder Miststück (als Bezeichnung für eine Frau) "She's a real bitch."; 2. beschissen (bezogen auf etwas) "Life's a bitch."; 3. abschätzige Bezeichnung für Frauen im allgemeinen; 4. (Verb) meckern

Bulldyke (Substantiv): eine betont maskuline Lesbierin (Dyke)

Bullshit (Substantiv): 1. Quatsch, Unsinn; 2. (Verb) jemand bescheißen; 3. plaudern; 4. Schaum schlagen

butt-ugly (Adjektiv): potthäßlich

Crabs (Substantiv): Filzläuse, Sackratten

Date (Substantiv): ein Rendezvous

Faggot (Substantiv): Schwuchtel, Tunte

French tickler (Substantiv): Kondom mit Noppen, Spikes und anderen luststeigernden (?!) Zu- bzw. Aufsätzen

Fuck: Wohl eines der vielseitigsten Wörter der englischen Sprache diesseits oder jenseits des Atlantiks. In seiner Grund-

bedeutung entspricht *fuck* "ficken" bzw "Fick" und wird genauso wie im Deutschen verwendet. Dabei ist nur auf die *Passive* bzw. *Active Voice* zu achten, d.h. wer fickt wen? Ansonsten kann *fuck* Ausdruck der Verärgerung, des Staunens oder sogar der Bewunderung sein und in beinahe jeder Lebenssituation verwendet werden. Der Umgang mit *fuck will* gelernt sein, denn der gleiche Ausdruck kann sowohl eine positive als auch eine negative Bedeutung haben. "Fuck you!" zum Beispiel, entspricht in etwa "Leck mich doch am Arsch!" und genau wie im Deutschen hängt die Bedeutung ganz vom Tonfall ab. Wird der Ausdruck scherzhaft unter Seinesgleichen verwendet, ist es keine Beleidigung. Man sollte aber davon absehen, ihn bei fremden Menschen anzuwenden, es sei denn der Gesprächspartner ist wesentlich kleiner als man selbst.
"Fuck me!" dagegen, oder "Well, I'll just be fucked!" beziehen sich eindeutig auf den Sprecher selbst und können genauso gut angewendet werden, wenn man erfährt, daß sein Auto geklaut worden ist oder daß man eine Million im Lotto gewonnen hat.
Ansonsten kann man *fuck* in fast jeden beliebigen Satz als Verstärkung der Sprachintention, z.B. als Imperativ einflechten:

Leave me alone!	Laß mich in Ruhe!
Leave me the fuck alone!	Laß mich verdammt noch mal in Ruhe!

(siehe auch: "the fucking genitive", und "question words with fuck")

Fuck-bunny (Substantiv): Bett-Häschen

fucked-up (Adjektiv): im Eimer; versaut; am Arsch; abgefuckt

fuck off and die: verpiß dich!

Hard-on (Substantiv): Erektion, Ständer

horny (Adjektiv): geil

Motherfucker: Da Inzest impliziert wird, wehren sich die Philologen vehement gegen eine wörtliche Übersetzung dieses Wortes. Zu Unrecht, wie Dr. McNaughety meint, denn nicht die eigene Mutter muß gemeint sein. Man denke etwa an das Lied von Neil Young "Welfare mothers make better lovers" (≅ Alleinerziehende Mütter sind die besseren Liebhaber). Wo auch immer die Ursprünge des Wortes liegen, *motherfucker* in seiner heutigen Bedeutung ist ein sehr schönes Wort, das *fuck* in seiner Vielseitigkeit in nichts nachsteht. Man kann *motherfuck* als Verb oder Adjektiv überall da einsetzen, wo man sonst *fuck* einsetzen würde und so seine *repartie* phantasievoll variieren.

Zum Beispiel, statt:

Fuck you!	Motherfuck you!
Fuck me!	Motherfuck me!
I'll be fucked!	I'll be motherfucked!
What fucking time is it?	What motherfucking time is it?

Die Bedeutung kann positiv oder negativ sein, je nach Betonung bzw. Kontext. So kann "a fine motherfucker" eine schöne

Frau bezeichnen. "A real motherfucker" dagegen bezeichnet eine beschissene Situation, Sache oder ein fieses Arschloch.

Auch als Substantiv werden *motherfucker / motherfuck* wie *fuck* verwendet. Nur in der Grundbeutung von "Kopulation" geht das nicht, d.h. wenn man im Deutschen "ficken" verwenden würde, kann man *motherfuck* nicht einsetzen.

Beispiele:

I don't give a fuck.	I don't give a motherfuck.
The test was a real fucker.	The test was a real motherfucker.

Nooner (Substantiv): Mittagsfick

Pearl necklace (Substantiv): eine Perlenkette (Liebesperlen)
"That's not jewelry she's talkin' about,
It really don't cost that much."
ZZ Top
"Pearl Necklace"

puke (Verb): 1. kotzen; 2. (Substantiv): Kotze

Quickie (Substantiv): eine schnelle Nummer

shit out of luck: Pech haben

shitty (Adjektiv): beschissen

Sleazebag (Substantiv): eine ekelhafte, versiffte Person

slutty (Adjektiv): nuttig

Stroke-book (Substantiv): ein Sex-Heft; Wichsvorlage

sucks: (bezogen auf etwas) beschissen, das Allerletzte. "This band sucks."

to catch some Z's: sich auf's Ohr legen; schlafen

to check (someone or something) out: sich ein Bild machen; sich informieren; sich etwas angucken

to cut the cheese: einen fahren lassen; furzen

to flash (Verb): sich blitzartig entblößen (Exhibitionismus)

to get one's balls in an uproar: sich aufregen

to give (someone) the finger: der Stinkefinger; die *digitus impudicus*-Geste

to give someone some shit: 1. jemanden verarschen, belügen; 2. jemanden ärgern

to give/not give a rat's ass: scheißegal "I could give a rat's ass"; "I don't give a rat's ass."

to hang out (Verb): herumhängen

to have a rod on: einen Ständer haben

to have a shit fit: ausrasten; die Krise kriegen

to monkey with something: an etwas herumfummeln

to pass out wolf tickets: Scheiße reden; jemanden durch leere Worte in Schach halten

to piss someone off: jemanden aufregen, ankotzen (Dr. McNaughety says: "It's better to be pissed off than pissed on.")

to put out (Verb): die Beine breit machen

to step on a duck (Verb): einen fahrenlassen; furzen

to take a whiz: urinieren; pissen

to upchuck (Verb): kotzen

Two-bagger: Ableitung von der Redewendung "She's so ugly, you have to put a bag over her head." Eine, die so häßlich ist, daß man vorsichtshalber zwei Tüten nimmt, falls die erste kaputtgeht. Auch von Frauen verwendet, um häßliche Männer zu bezeichnen

Weenie-wagger (Substantiv): Exhibitionist

Wimp (Substantiv): ein halbes Hemd; Schlappschwanz